SIX (+2) ESSAYS

JESSICA
HELFAND

six(+2)
essays
on
design
and
new
media

WILLIAM
DRENTTEL
NEW YORK
1997

EXPANDED EDITION—1997
ISBN 1 884381 13 8 paper

FIRST EDITION—1995
ISBN 1 884381 08 1 cloth
ISBN 1 884381 09 X paper

Essays originally published in *Print* and *Eye* Magazines 1994–1997

FOR MALCOLM

contents

1

THE ESSAYS IN THIS BOOK ARE NOT ABOUT COMPUTERS. They are not about downloading software or upgrading hardware. They will not discuss 3-D rendering or animation tools or special effects. (At least not intentionally.) They will not report on mergers, takeovers and buyouts in the telecommunications industry. (At least not directly.) They will try to avoid lingo and computer-speak, references to RAM and ROM and acronyms of all kinds. Their mission—and mine—is to look at the ideas that are shaping and being shaped by the rapid growth of information technologies, both within the design profession and throughout the world. Their primary goal is to examine ideas that illuminate new kinds of thinking: new content (how the evolution of technology in a global economy informs our ideas); new visions (the ways in which those ideas become physically manifest); new challenges (understanding the permutations of sound, space and time, particularly in interactive media); new skills (formal, functional, conceptual, ideological); new audiences (multi-lingual, multi-cultural and multi-disciplinary); and most importantly, new questions: questions about form and content, about process and product, about creativity, collaboration and craft. My goal is to debunk the jargon and demystify the trends, to ask penetrating as well as provocative questions, and to show work that goes beyond the predictable parameters of the computer screen: work that even in the so-called digital era demonstrates real creativity—the triumph of reason over reaction, of imagination over technique.

A prominent designer confessed to me recently that he had finally broken down and purchased Adobe Photoshop for his studio."We have, however, issued a mandate," he was quick to point out, "that it be used responsibly—not to manipulate images." He then described the sheer delight experienced by his colleagues as they booted up, viewing their very first scanned image on the virgin Photoshop screen. "We drew mustaches on Santa Claus," he reported gleefully. "It was fun."

Fun, it seems, is an occupational hazard for most designers, and a behavior essential to design-gone-digital. It is, after all, part of an enduring and distinguished legacy: both Paul Rand (*Design and the Play Instinct*) and Bradbury Thompson (*Type as a Toy*) were early advocates of the usefulness of play in design. "There is no creative aspect of graphic design more enjoyable or rewarding," wrote Thompson, "than the indulgence in play." Play, too, is a welcome and much-needed antidote to the dryness that technology only too often suggests. If we submit to the inclination to be playful, even mischievous where screen-based images are concerned, it is largely a consequence of our expectations. Image programs, like Adobe Photoshop, offer a plethora of choices—brushes and filters, pens and pencils, masks and erasers. Look at all those tools, all those toys! Think about it: if you were standing in front of the Mona Lisa and someone handed you a can of spray paint, inviting you to go wild—telling you that anything you did, any alteration or defacement could instantly be erased—wouldn't you be just the least bit tempted?

It is precisely this element of play, and the momentary empowerment it entails, that emboldens us, challenges us, and in some cases, corrupts us. Such are some of the goofier characteristics of this new technology—technology that permits, even encourages modifications and maneuvers unindulged in the unforgiving world of paper. On screen, we acquire augmented powers: we can dupe and distort, flip and flop, colorize and compress and recreate an image at will. But do we? Should we? Who decides, and how? And when?

The hope is that we will behave responsibly, and not abuse the privileges that design-on-the-desktop has introduced. But sometimes we falter. We make mistakes. We experiment. We play. We take the sorts of risks we might not take were we not in the presence of a computer. Conversely, the absence of the computer may, in certain cases, be advisable and may lead to equally experimental processes; it is the nature of the exploration that is different, not the exploration itself.

Ironically, despite the practicality with which it is most frequently identified, the computer adds an unusual element of serendipity to the creative process. Its role is unclear, its contribution uncertain. It remains an unknown quantity, its qualifications undefined. Can it be more than a word processor, more than a production tool, more than a machine? What is it, really, and how does it fit in? And where, incidentally, is it headed?

The reality is that none of us really know just how far it's going to take us. Most of us agree that the computer won't think for us, but we continue to wonder: can it engage us—creatively, conceptually—to the degree that it modifies our thinking?

In the best of circumstances, the play instinct leads us toward improvisation. We fire and miss, revert to saved and fire again. The screen becomes an endlessly forgiving sketching surface—gone is the anxiety of 'ruining' the blank first page of a brand-new sketchbook. Here, variations can be saved, saved-as, renamed and saved again, imported into alternate programs and reinvented altogether. Magically, our near-misses are exceptionally easy to erase. Maybe too easy.

In the worst of circumstances, we stop thinking. Creativity is suppressed by the thrill of novelty, supplanted by the tempting lure of endless possibilities. It is worth noting that the very abundance of possibilities is one of the computer's greatest virtues, but only—as Paul Rand points out in his excellent book, *Design, Form and Chaos*—in the hands of a thoughtful designer. Thoughtless computer-aided (or driven) design maximizes shortcuts. It delights in gimmickry and exploits for effect. Here, in the land of the gratuitous filter, it is a virtual celebration of bells and whistles, uninspired form and negligible content. Surely you've seen this type of work: brightly colored geometric solids rotating endlessly through space, garish palettes, distorted typography. This is the play instinct gone awry—devoid of imagination, brain-free, giving way to the loathsome gravitational pull of mediocrity.

Although it is an undeniably elitist argument, this is one of the things that separate designers (and here I am referring to good designers) from the rest of the world: ideally, we possess both a discerning mind and a discriminating eye—not to mention a certain modicum of responsibility, at least where our work is concerned. Indeed, the computer forces us to rethink the moral underpinnings of our aesthetic choices. Questions of authorship, ownership and originality are pervasive. As we migrate toward multimedia, where our work resides in and is distributed by uniquely digital means, the potential for plagiarism is huge. How do we legislate, or even begin to identify, guidelines—formal, functional, ethical—in this environment? There are those who have argued that one of the more unfortunate aspects of our profession is the fact that one need not be certified to practice. Add to this the ethical free-for-all that quickly ensues in the world of electronic data, and the demand for integrity has never been greater, or more critical.

Arguments for and against the morality of digital photography have become equally complex, as we struggle to understand what is advisable, permissible and indeed, appropriate. It is, oddly enough, a rights issue—not unlike the abortion debate, in the sense that what ultimately remains undecided is the moment at which life (in this case, the life of the photograph) begins. Here, digital images are at odds with more traditional methodologies, and computer-based software programs, purportedly designed as extensions to the traditional darkroom, are perceived as the invasive enemies of a purist aesthetic. Conversely, one might argue that the very nature of photography itself depends upon processes which are by definition manipulations of a singular vision—aperture, film and shutter speed, processing time—all of which help to shape the final form. In this rationale, the computer is understood to be part of a greater, more comprehensive gestalt, one that identifies technology as an integral component in an overall creative process.

The great promise of computers in general (and, I might add, multimedia in particular) lies in their ability to enhance the way we communicate with one another and with the technology that serves us. Is a computer merely a tool? Is it an international language? A boon or an impediment to creativity? Can we use computers to come up with new ideas, or merely to execute existing ones? Reports differ, but what remains true is the degree to which we are coming to depend upon them—in our banks, our museums, our supermarkets, our airports and train terminals, our schools and libraries, our offices and our homes.

For designers, the computer is, in effect, the canvas of the twenty-first century. It touches everything we do. It intrigues us, captivates us, puzzles us. It frustrates us. But one thing is certain: it is not going to go away. What we do with it, how we employ its potential and deploy our own, will have significant and far-reaching consequences for the entire design profession, and will ultimately help to determine ways in which we might push technology—and ourselves—even further.

2

IN 1968, MATTEL INTRODUCED TALKING BARBIE.
I like to think of this as my first computer. I remember saving up
my allowance for what seemed an eternity to buy one. To make
her talk, you pulled a little string; upon its release, slave-to-fash-
ion Barbie would utter delightful little conversational quips like "I
think mini-skirts are smashing" and "Let's have a costume party."

If you held the string back slightly as she was talking, her
voice would drop a few octaves, transforming her from a chirpy
soprano into a slurpy baritone. What came out then sounded a lot
more like "Let's have a cocktail party."

I loved that part. What I loved was playing director—casting
her in a new role, assigning her a new (albeit ludicrous) personality. I loved controlling the tone of her voice, altering the rhythm
of her words, modulating her oh-so-minimal (and moronic)
vocabulary. I loved having the power to shape her language—
something I would later investigate typographically, as I strug-
gled to understand the role of the printed word as an emissary of
spoken communication.

Twenty-five years later, my Macintosh sounds a lot like my
Barbie did then—the same monotone, genderless, robotic drawl.

But here in the digital age, the relationship between design and sound—and in particular, between the spoken word and the written word—goes far beyond pulling a string. The truth is that the computer's internal sound capabilities enable us to design with sound, not just in imitation of it. Like it or not, the changes brought about by recent advances in technology (and here I am referring primarily to interactive media) indicate the need for designers to broaden their understanding of what it is to work effectively with typography. It is no longer enough to design for readability, to suggest a sentiment or reinforce a concept through the selection of a particular font. Today, we can make type talk: in any language, at any volume, with musical underscoring or sci-fi sound effects or overlapping violins. We can sequence and dissolve, pan and tilt, fade to black and specify type in sensurround. As we "set" type, we encounter a decision-making process unprecedented in two-dimensional design: unlike the kinetic experience of turning a printed page to sequence information, here, *time* becomes a powerful and per-suasive design element. Today, we can visualize concepts in four action-packed, digital dimensions.

Interactive media have introduced a new visual language, one that is no longer bound to traditional definitions of word and image, form and place. Typography, in an environment that offers such diverse riches, must redefine its goals, its purpose, its very identity. It must reinvent itself. And soon.

Visual language, or the interpretation of spoken words through typographic expression, has long been a source of inspiration to artists and writers. Examples abound, dating as far back as the incunabula and extending upwards from concrete poetry in the '20s to 'happenings' in the '60s to today's multicultural morass of pop culture. Visual wordplay proliferates, in this century in particular, from F.T. Marinetti's *Parole in Libertà* to George Maciunas' *Fluxus* installations to the latest MTA posters adorning New York subway walls. Kurt Schwitters, Guillaume Apollinaire, Piet Zwart, Robert Brownjohn—the list is long, the examples inexhaustible. For designers there has always been an overwhelming interest in formalism, in analyzing the role of type as medium (structure), message (syntax), and muse (sensibility). Throughout, there has been an attempt to reconcile the relationship between words both spoken and seen—a source of exhilaration to some and ennui to others. Lamenting the expressive limitations of the western alphabet, Adolf Loos explained it simply: "One cannot *speak* a capital letter." Denouncing its structural failings, Stanley Morrison was equally at odds with a tradition that designated hierarchies in the form of upper and lowercase letterforms. Preferring to shape language as he deemed appropriate, Morrison referred to caps as "a necessary evil."

Academic debate over the relationship between language and form has enjoyed renewed popularity in recent years as designers borrow from linguistic models in an attempt to codify—and clarify—their own typographic explorations. Deconstruction's design devotées have eagerly appropriated its terminology and theory, hoping to introduce a new vocabulary for design: it is the vocabulary of signifiers and signifieds, of Jacques Derrida and Ferdinand de Saussure, of Michel Foucault and Umberto Eco.

As a comprehensive model for evaluating typographic expression, deconstruction has ultimately proved both heady and limited. Today, as advances in technology introduce greater and more complex creative challenges, it is simply arcane. We need to look at screen-based typography as a new language, with its own grammar, its own syntax and its own rules. What we need are new and better models, models that go beyond language or typography per se, and that reinforce rather than restrict our understanding of what it is to design with electronic media: what Wendy Richmond has called "extreme and unusual metaphors."

Learning a new language is one thing, fluency quite another. Yet we've come to equate fluency with literacy—another outdated model for evaluation. "Literacy should not mean the ability to decode strings of alphabetic letters," says Seymour Papert, Director of the Epistemology and Learning Group at the MIT Media Lab, who refers to such a definition as "letteracy." And language, even to linguists, proves creatively limiting as a paradigm. "New media promise the opportunity to offer a smoother transition to what really deserves to be called literacy," says Papert. Typography, as the physical embodiment of such thinking, has quite a way to go.

The will to decipher the formal properties of language, a topic of great consequence for communication designers in general, has its philosophical antecedents in ancient Greece. "Spoken words," wrote Aristotle in *Logic*, "are the symbols of mental experience. Written words are the symbols of spoken words." Today, centuries later, the equation has added a new link: what happens when written words can speak? When they can move? When they can be imbued with sound and tone and nuance and decibel and harmony and voice? As designers probing the creative parameters of this new technology, our goal may be less to digitize than to dramatize. Indeed, there is a theatrical component that I am convinced is essential to this new thinking. Of what value are typographic choices—bold and italics, for example—when words can dance across the screen, dissolve, or disappear altogether?

In this dynamic landscape, our static definitions of typography appear increasingly imperiled. Will the beauty of traditional letterforms be compromised by the evils of this new technology? Will punctuation be stripped of its functional contributions, or ligatures their aesthetic ones? Will type really matter?

Of course it will.

In the meantime, however, typography's early appearance on the digital frontier doesn't bode well for design. Take e-mail, for example. Gone are the days of good handwriting, of the Palmer Method and the penmanship primer. In its place, electronic mail which, despite its futuristic tone, has paradoxically revived the antiquated art of letter writing. Sending e-mail is easy and effortless and quick. For those of us who spend a good deal of our professional lives on the telephone, it offers a welcome respite from talking, and, consequently, bears a closer stylistic resemblance to conversational speech than to written language. However, for those of us with even the most modest design sense, it eliminates the distinctiveness that typography has traditionally brought to our written communiqués. Though its supporters endorse the democratic nature of such homogeneity, the truth is, it's boring. In the land of e-mail, we all "sound" alike: everyone writes in system fonts.

E-mail is laden with such contradictions: ubiquitous in form yet highly diverse in content, at once ephemeral and archival, transmitted in real time yet physically intangible. E-mail is a kind of aesthetic flatland, informationally dense and visually unimaginative. Here, hierarchies are preordained and nonnegotiable: passwords, menus, commands, help. Commercial services like America Online require that we title our mail, a leftover model from the days of interoffice correspondence, which makes even the most casual letter sound like a corporate memo. As a result, electronic missives all have headlines: titling our letters makes us better editors, not better designers. As a fitting metaphor for the distilled quality of things digital, the focus in e-mail is on the abridged, the acronym, the quick read. E-mail is functionally serviceable and visually forgettable, not unlike fast food. It's drive-through design: get in, get out, move on.

And it's everywhere. Here is the biggest contribution to communication technology to come out of the last decade, a global network linking some millions of people worldwide, and designers— communication designers, no less—are nowhere in sight.

Typography, in this environment, desperately needs direction. Where to start? Comparisons with printed matter inevitably fail, as words in the digital domain are processed with a speed unprecedented in the world of paper. Here, they are incorporated into databases or interactive programs, where they are transmitted and accessed in random, nonhierarchical sequences. "Hypertext," or the ability to program text with interactivity— meaning that a word, when clicked upon or pointed to will, in fact, do something—takes it all a step further: here, by introducing alternate paths, information lacks the closure of the traditional printed narrative. "Hypertextual story space is now multidimensional," explains Robert Coover in the magazine *Artforum,* "and theoretically infinite."

If graphic design can be largely characterized by its attention to understanding the hierarchy of information (and using type in accordance with such understanding), then how are we to determine its use in a nonlinear context such as this? On a purely visual level, we are limited by what the pixel will render: the screen matrix simulates curves with surprising sophistication, but hairlines and serifs will, to the serious typophile, appear inevitably compromised. On a more objective level, type in this context is both silent and static, and must compete with sound and motion—not an easy task, even in the best of circumstances. Conversely, in the era of the handheld television remote, where the user can—and does—mute at will, the visual impact of written typography is not to be discounted.

To better analyze the role(s) of electronic typography, we might begin by looking *outside*: not to remote classifications imported from linguistic textbooks, or even to traditional design theories conveniently repackaged, but to our own innate intelligence and distinctive powers of creative thought. To cultivate and adequately develop this new typography (because if we don't, no one else will), we might do well to rethink visual language altogether, to consider new and alternative perspectives. "If language is indeed the limit of our world," writes literary critic William Gass in *Habitations of the Word*, "then we must find another, larger, stronger, more inventive language which will burst those limits."

In his book *Seeing Voices*, author and neurologist Oliver Sacks reflects on the complexity of sign language, and describes the cognitive understanding of spatial grammar in a language that exists without sound. He cites the example of a deaf child learning to sign, and details the remarkable quality of her visual awareness and descriptive, spatial capabilities. "By the age of four, indeed, Charlotte had advanced so far into visual thinking and language that she was able to provide new ways of think-ing—revelations—to her parents." As a consequence of learning sign language as adults, this particular child's parents not only learned a new language, but discovered new ways of thinking as well—visual thinking. Imagine the potential for interactive media if designers were to approach electronic typography with this kind of ingenuity and openmindedness.

William Stokoe, a Chaucer scholar who taught Shakespeare at Gallaudet College in the 1950s, summarized it this way: "In a signed language, narrative is no longer linear and prosaic. Instead, the essence of sign language is to cut from a normal view to a close-up to a distant shot to a close-up again, and so on, even including flashback and fast-forward scenes, exactly as a movie editor works." Here, perhaps, is another model for visual thinking: a new way of shaping meaning based on multiple points of view, which sees language as part of a more comprehensive communication platform—time-sensitive, interactive and highly visual. Much like multimedia.

3

THE
PLEASURE
OF THE
TEXT[URE]

RIDLEY SCOTT'S *BLADE RUNNER* WAS RELEASED IN 1983. In this filmic adaptation of the 1969 Phillip Dick thriller, *Do Androids Dream of Electric Sheep?*, the terrain swells with shiny metals and smoky steel, futuristic renderings of imagined experience, mesmerizing—and what might appropriately be termed classic science fiction. Organically interactive, it is a graphic design tour-de-force of motion and emotion, fear and fantasy, with indeed, no shortage of drama. Critically acclaimed for its brilliant visualizations, *Blade Runner* crafted a polymorphous landfill with tricky edges and spurs, a world rich in what today's multimedia developers might call look and feel: so rich, in fact, that it caused one reviewer to ask: is the texture overwhelming the text?

Richard Corliss's review in *Time* magazine credited the visionary Scott with bringing the story to life by weaving an intricate narrative web that included, but wasn't driven by, its text. Today, as we journey through the layers of electronic information that we call multimedia—literally, the convergence of technologies to create new modes of expression—the role of information is being increasingly redefined. Like Ridley Scott's film, today's data-intensive environment is without rules or boundaries. But unlike the *Blade Runner* model, most multimedia is also without texture. It is often overmapped, underdesigned, and anonymous—an information flatland. In an effort to simplify our navigation through vast amounts of data, texture itself is often eliminated altogether, rendering complex content through inappropriately simple means. In screen-based media, the results so far are dull and disappointing indeed.

In pursuit of texture, and in the spirit of extending the creative boundaries that so narrowly constrain this medium, students at MIT's Visible Language Workshop are exploring new theoretical models that challenge the structure of the much-touted information highway. "Consider instead," they suggest, "an information landscape." They propose "an interactive and dynamic universe of worlds with landscapes of typographic, spatial and symbolic information." In this view, the topology of multimedia has enormous texture, and the ideology of multimedia has enormous promise. But at present, such models remain the exception rather than the rule. Today's commercial offerings in interactive multimedia lack the sophistication of this thinking, and consequently, the market is flooded with products that reveal little in the way of design excellence.

Texture—and here I am referring not to surface texture but to texture as multiple levels of experience—is complexity made physically manifest. Multimedia, overflowing with complexity (and driven by the user's own unpredictable experience), mostly appears to be anything but. Organized along linear pathways and Cartesian coordinates, many multimedia products take us on journeys through dense forests of information as though navigating a city with chronologically numbered streets. Form, which in this case is still being formed, is increasingly at odds with the content from which it stems.

In an overwhelming effort to clarify, texture itself is often greatly diminished, if not altogether destroyed. Pictographic wayfinding systems become organizational straitjackets, driven by buttons and menus and arrows. But why? Such approaches breed sterile interfaces, environments that undermine interactive media by compromising the very complexity that is its richest asset. Why not probe the conceptual dimensions of this new design space? Why not invent other new worlds to explore?

The invention of new worlds is precisely what is needed. In the ten years since the introduction of the Macintosh, we have witnessed the evolution of an international language, a visual vocabulary consisting of metaphors for lived experience in the form of primitive hieroglyphics. The precursor to all this was Xerox's Star Interface, developed in 1981; its positive contribution lay in the simple premise that most people who use computers lack the experience to operate them. Its downfall lay in its limited aesthetic model: the "desktop" remains the ubiquitous hallmark of this questionable legacy.

With a visual identity comprised of file folders and miniature trashcans, the "desktop" mirrored our behaviors and represented our presumed needs in the truncated, rectangular arena of the screen. Over time, this icon-based vocabulary became a means to bridge the gulf between art and science, between culture and language, between today and tomorrow and the next millenium. The notion that multimedia can both anticipate and archive information that is constantly changing is but one of many myths perpetuated by an industry that is still young enough to generate enthusiasm at the expense of truth. And sadly, it would seem, at the expense of good design as well.

Design (such as it was) and its multimedia variants grew from this vocabulary. Though language-independent and therefore marketable on a global scale, icons eventually became static organizational tools, distilling information into its most salient but often most boring form. The same "camera" icon, for example, might activate a Popeye animation, a World War II film clip and a Playboy video calendar. In this view, icons remain dispassionate observers of the diversified environments they serve. Here, the "landscape" is bifurcated: icons are relegated to a separate picture plane (foreground) from content (background). From this perspective, navigation tools are generic ushers, not integrated protagonists.

Conversely, the very ability to access filmic material at all remains one of the great promises of new media. The stories we tell assume greater scope and meaning. The order in which such stories are heard or read or experienced are, for the most part, beyond the designer's hierarchical control. The very nature of interactivity increases memory retention. What will users take away with them when they walk away from the computer screen?

The aesthetic, such as it is, needs help. Structured "paths" and their attendant icons resemble the anonymous supergraphics of the 1970s: clean, colorful, and characterless, they telegraph the banal visual vernacular of computerese. But in the multimedia environment, paths tend to proliferate, growing exponentially and turning clarity into confusion as the web of information grows larger, increasing the number of choices we make and leaving to us the order in which we make them. Control or chaos?

Empowerment or anxiety? Either is possible, but what is becoming increasingly clear is the degree to which the success of a given product lies in achieving a balance between the two.

In their haste to organize often unrelated types of media, many multimedia products oversimplify the design experience, creating linear templates for decidedly nonlinear material. With enough of these products on the market, the general public has quickly grown accustomed to such conventions, to following the icons, to navigating along such preordained paths. Inadvertently, perhaps, we have automated this process into three successive tasks: point, click, surrender.

In one of the earliest interactive offerings on the CD-ROM market, interactive maps and video clips help illustrate a courageous woman's journey through the Australian outback. Rick Smolan's *From Alice to Ocean* keeps us just on the periphery of the narrative, ready to "click on Rick" to access photo tips and confirm shutter speeds. Experiential or informational? Multimedia, as in this case, often aspires to be both, and the disparity between inside (experiential) and outside (informational) reflects an identity crisis that characterizes much of this industry.

And it is an enormous industry, including interface design (referred to frequently as "graphical user interface design," literally designing the connection between the software and the person operating it); interactive design (human factors design, often involving extensive usability studies to determine better product performance); and more complex tasks that demand greater computer fluency—programming in code, for example, which tends to be a rarity for most classically trained designers. Says Robin Baker, professor of computing at London's Royal College of

Art: "Multimedia design raises issues of metaphor, types of representation, cognition, sound, movement, graphics and text—demanding a range of skills that do not normally form part of the education of graphic and industrial designers." He credits the emergence of the collaborative team as a necessary step in formulating a structure within which multimedia design can successfully take shape. "To provide the density of solution that is required, alongside the designer will be the cognitive scientist, the psychologist, the filmmaker and the software engineer."

Like "texture" and the "information landscape," Baker's "density of solution" model is another way of articulating the richness that multimedia, as more than just the sum of its parts, seems destined to achieve. Under the direction of Gillian Crampton-Smith, students in the Computer-Related Design course at London's Royal College of Art concentrate on integrating "the poetic with the practical." Crampton-Smith believes that multimedia is a "creative discipline which will shape the electronic environment of the future." Her focus, and that of her students, is to forge a new language of interactive design: "Engineers have been concentrating on how to make these technologies work; [designers] are good at thinking what should be designed to provide rich and satisfying experiences in their everyday use."

In many multimedia projects, though, design is perceived as only one aspect of the process, and not always a critical one. And rarely is it considered imperative at the initiating stages of a project. Design, in this view, is palliative rather than prescriptive, and therein lies the problem.

So who designs these products? There are game designers, software designers, interface designers, production designers, programming designers, and occasionally, even graphic designers. In most multimedia settings, the designer is the person with the vision, not necessarily the person who is visual. The "designer" can be the author, publisher, producer, or even programmer.

The misuse, overuse and flagrant abuse of the term "designer" is not going to go away. Like "creatives" in advertising, professional designers hoping for certified designation in interactive multimedia may be disappointed. Because multimedia production is driven by forces which, though creative in intent, are not primarily visual in nature, the role of designer in this new medium remains to be invented.

And yet, in order for this medium to succeed, certain critical issues remain to be addressed, issues largely pertaining to the very nature of communication design. The beauty of this technology (if it exists at all) lies in its ability to combine text not only with images, but also with sound, animation and video. In its ideal state, multimedia is a well-oiled machine with perfectly synchronized gears, a fusion of disparate elements that together reinforce our understanding of a particular topic by virtue of their symphonic interrelation.

Success, though, is relative. Multimedia is still in its infancy, and its fledgling profit margin reflects the uncertainty of a market that is still trying desperately to define itself. Though often evaluated by publishing standards, its numbers are significantly lower than might be expected: most CD-ROMs sell fewer than 5000 copies. Even Peter Gabriel's *Xplora*, which reportedly cost over $1 million to produce, has only sold somewhere in the neighborhood of 20,000 copies. Voyager, an early multimedia pioneer and one of the nation's most prolific publishers of electronic books, laserdiscs, and academically inspired software, sells most of its products in the neighborhood of 5,000 to 25,000 copies (its one exception is the Beatles' remix of *A Hard Day's Night*). The company, however, has yet to turn a profit since its inception over a decade ago.

Nonetheless, multimedia remains a substantial market: total CD-ROM title sales in 1993 reached $102 million, with a total of 8 million discs sold. Mega-publisher Microsoft reported total sales this same year of $4 billion—two-thirds the gross receipts of the entire Hollywood movie industry (and just a scant $246 billion less than this year's national defense budget). With substantial capital to invest and storytelling talent to boot, Hollywood is looking more and more like the next multimedia frontier: indeed, for movie moguls aspiring to become software developers, PowerBooks are said to have supplanted personal trainers as the newest emblems of chic and exalted status.

Piqued by the software feeding frenzy in the entertainment business, music executives, too, are looking to boost record and ticket sales through this new medium. But for the musicians themselves, the goal is to probe the artistry of the new interactive tools. While singers like Peter Gabriel and David Bowie are releasing CD-ROMs that strategically play to their fan base by inviting users to take studio tours and re-mix their own recordings, the true and unrivaled leader in this field is Brian Eno. In his book *Cyberia*, author Douglas Rushkoff describes Eno's distinctive impact on interactive music. "Internally, Eno's music isn't a set of particular sounds one listens to but a space in which one breathes. These aren't songs with beginnings and endings, but extended moments—almost static experiences."

For Eno, design for interactivity has an improvisational quality. He believes our efforts are best served by taking a broader, more comprehensive view of the material and composing the means by which it is presented and subsequently experienced. "It's not all tightly organized," he explains. "It's a network rather than a structure." In Rushkoff's view, Eno's vision "paved the way for Macintosh musicians by taking the emphasis off structure and placing it on texture."

Eno's latest project is a collaboration with Laurie Anderson and Peter Gabriel to create an interactive theme park, a giant web of rides and activities and dynamic, interactive games. In the spirit of the information landscape, *Real World Experience Park* is committed to demystifying technology so that users become active, contributing participants. Laurie Anderson describes it as a "nursery for hybrids." Peter Gabriel imagines it as a "magic garden." For Brian Eno, it is an "anti-zoo, an urban tom-tom, a visionary playground."

This notion takes interactivity as a passive ideal and makes it truly active. A generation ago, social theorist Ivan Illych described this as "convivial" media: the idea of users adding to and not just taking. Soon, interactive media will have the capacity to do just this. And increasingly, as technology evolves to support greater community interaction—from networked on-line communication systems to advances in virtual reality—projects like Eno's virtual theme park will become a distinct reality.

And the theme park has the added attraction of being essentially game-based. In their purest sense, games have been a mainstay of the multimedia market since the very beginning. Recreational and inherently interactive, they have traditionally been packaged as instructional software—from soccer to canasta to 3-dimensional golf. Ironically, however, the really successful games ignore the prevailing "organized" trend and exploit the very technology that, we are told, "good" interface design should try to make invisible. Making no attempt to conceal their complexity (a good thing), these games tend to be button-heavy and graphically congested (a bad thing), include extensive sound resources and complex 3-dimensional imaging, and are themed to topics like flight-simulation and drag racing. Plot-driven and on the violent side, most of these games are a cross between television cop shows and watered-down Nintendo games, cartoon versions of techno-terror masquerading as action-packed drama: this isn't texture—it's graphic turbulence. While some might argue a dramatic debt to a certain sci-fi movie mentioned earlier, the reality is, they are locked in the model of the pinball arcade. And, small wonder, they are geared to a market that is predominantly male and under 40.

And here, the numbers skyrocket: *Rebel Assault*, a George Lucas Production, sold 250,000 copies in its first month. Virgin Entertainment's *Seventh Guest* sold over 500,000 copies in one year. Brøderbund's much-publicized *Myst*, did even better: a decidedly less violent interactive odyssey, *Myst* includes some 2,500 photo-realistic images as well as its own original soundtrack. Ultimately, it succeeds because of its theatricality: in the words of one reviewer, *Myst* is "part movie, part dream."

Called "the *War and Peace* of multimedia" by Rolling Stone critic Jon Katz, *Myst* is big: travelling through its multiple paths could take days. Which brings up an added benefit of CD-ROM technology: space. With adequate room, multimedia can include multiple resources, choices, possibilities and interconnections. It also affords extensive archiving, indexing, and keyword searching, functions of something called hypertext which allows for the designation of a word or idea as a launch pad to some further annotation. Hypertext isn't new: the phrase was coined by Theodor Holm Nelson some 30-odd years ago, and the concept itself has been around since the mid-1940's, when *Atlantic Monthly* ran an article by Vannevar Bush, Franklin Roosevelt's science advisor at the time, stressing the need for more sophisticated cross-referencing capabilities in data retrieval systems. Hypertext remains the most compelling (and indeed, enduring) feature of interactive multimedia precisely because it stems from an idea—that of linking by association instead of by indexing— rather than from any pre-conceived structure per se.

If hypertext exists to support nonsequential thinking, then the function of multimedia may be to supplement this thinking with additional, complex resources—resources that, at present, are most efficiently packaged in compact disk form. But this, too, is likely to change.

What does compact disk technology really have to offer? As a storage system, a single CD-ROM can hold the equivalent of about 330,000 pages of text, but only about 45 minutes of video footage. CD-ROMs are, to the best of our knowledge, archival. They are economical from a manufacturing standpoint, and less destructive, environmentally speaking, than their paper equivalents. But there are limits. Multimedia products demand more of us, and more of our computers. They can, and do, crash our systems. They can be excruciatingly slow: design in "real time" is still a fantasy. Video footage, digitized via Quicktime technology for integration into Macintosh software applications, is seriously limited in compression, frame rate, file size, duration and, depending on the calibration and configuration of one's monitor, resolution. Despite these limitations, such multimedia movies are perhaps best understood as their own peculiar genre—choppy and arrhythmic and primitive, they bear a closer resemblance to early Max Fleischer cartoons than to anything even remotely approximating the sophistication of broadcast quality.

From a design perspective, Quicktime "windows" can be structured so that users can move them around the screen (so much for design: it is impossible to predict where they will fall and what impact their placement will have on the configuration of other elements "designed" on the screen). Or they can reside squarely in a certain area of the screen—as in, for instance, Voyager's *Poetry in Motion*, a CD-ROM anthology of contemporary verse that operates from the simple premise of making poetry more resonant by illuminating the relationships between spoken and written words. In its best moments, our appreciation of a poetic phrase is enhanced by sound—literally, the opportunity to hear the lyrical cadences of writers like Michael Ondaatje and Tom Waits as they recite their poetry aloud. Conversely, an annoying transcript of each poem parallels these live readings, with no way to turn them off. It's pointless and unnecessary, like a kind of close-captioned multimedia for the imagination-impaired.

Rarely does a CD-ROM celebrate its technical limitations in pursuit of greater creative gain, as for instance, in Art Spiegelman's *Maus: A Survivor's Tale* (also published by Voyager). For the CD-ROM version, Spiegelman's wife, Françoise Mouly, videotaped him at Auschwitz with a handheld camera.

Interspersed throughout the program are clips of wobbly footage, many of them without sound: they are unpretentious and surprisingly moving. As an extension of the tale itself, these clips supplement the story by offering glimpses of the prison camp as it looks today, barren and strangely still. The rough footage enriches the texture and adds somehow to the poignancy of this story. It's low-tech and unpolished, and it's terrific.

Like many CD-ROMs, however, *Maus* runs from Hypercard, which, as an authoring system, possesses the dubious advantage of enabling large quantities of text to be sequenced, or "poured," into the program; consequently, its pacing is very book-like and, frankly, excruciatingly slow. Deciphering the schematic diagrams that take you through Spiegelman's sketches is confusing, making sense of the linear narrative amidst multiple levels of sound, video, and image even more so. Yet gradually you become acquainted with its texture, and somewhere along the line, your visit starts to mirror certain aspects of the author's own journey. Because it is a highly personal story, the focus is anchored by Spiegelman's rather idiosyncratic vision. The orchestration of additional narrative features (diaries, sketchbooks and so on) builds upon that vision to create an environment at once immersive and suggestive—of time and place, of character, of tragedy, of family.

Though *Maus* has its problems, it remains compelling because it is fueled by a very specific and highly personal vision. And here is an important distinction: although its production is by necessity team-driven, multimedia is best served when the underlying vision is a singular one. It is in the authorship—not the authoring tools—that such work becomes possible.

Single-subject documentaries such as these represent just one aspect of the multimedia industry. The bulk of CD-ROM title revenue, however, lies in reference materials. As a category, these CD-ROMs are an information design nightmare: the material is dense and text-intensive, organized into a collapsible (keyword-searchable) framework, and targeted to an often unknown audience with a correspondingly eclectic demographic profile.

One such product is *Time* magazine's CD-ROM *Almanac*. This is a prime example of generic multimedia—a poorly designed, clumsy and undistinguished interface. But breaking it down to its component parts yields an interesting design analysis, one that illuminates some of the more critical features facing interactive media design and designers.

Complete with weekly coverage from the last four years, the *Almanac* is supplemented with additional material dating as far back as Prohibition. Users can search by specific subject or by decade, or browse through additional media samples consisting mostly of video clips or wire service photos. Owing to its largely political nature, an additional feature to search by elections is included as well.

The *Almanac* works best and fastest when searching through text only. Much of the navigation exists as pull-down menus, which often makes logical leaps seem laborious and illogical. Video footage ranges from the pristine CNN variety (where broadcasters narrate in well-rehearsed voiceover—in direct contrast, it should be noted, to the immediacy of the allegedly newsworthy incident they're recounting) to random portions of what appear to be arbitrarily chosen interviews, to exquisitely constructed mini-documentaries.

One pull-down menu option allows for individualized font selection, enabling users to read an article in Caslon, Keedy Sans, or even, heaven forbid, Wiesbaden Swing. I found this attention to typographic flexibility of interest, particularly since the CD-ROM itself makes no attempt to match the design of its interface to the design of the magazine. As magazines look ahead to electronic distribution—literally, to circulation via networked online services—the relationship between a paper magazine and its digital variant will no doubt be examined more closely, and will hopefully yield more promising results than those in evidence here.

The *Almanac*'s interface engages aggressively in something called nesting: files in folders within files in folders, or the necessity to backtrack step by step to go to another section. Navigation becomes quickly tiresome in this environment: it's simply too much work. Ultimately, this structure testifies to the limitations of matrix-like mapping schemes.

The *Almanac* works best with hypertext links. I did a keyword search in its introductory menu, choosing words (like "multimedia," for example) pertinent to this article, and found source listings that allowed me to go back and locate every instance in which these words had been used over the past four years.

But in searching by decade, I came across another, more interesting level of information. Clicking on the Eisenhower icon for the 1950s, I found an article about the cobalt bomb, an aggressive cancer treatment developed by a group of Canadian atomic scientists some forty years ago. A button at the bottom of that screen displayed links to selected pieces of 1950s ephemera, as well as other articles from that decade with related technological references—a circuitous, but ultimately rewarding way to do research. My understanding of the early years of computer technology was thus enhanced by learning about the cobalt bomb: unrelated in topic, but related in time, I stumbled on a sampling of popular culture within which my chosen topic was more realistically positioned and, in the end, better understood.

It is this kind of annotated learning that makes user-directed, interactive media a compelling educational tool. Yet as the world's supply of information grows larger, CD-ROMs quickly become an insufficient means to archive and disseminate materials and are, for that matter, considered by many to be only a "bridge" technology— soon to be rendered obsolete by the next big advance in telecommunications.

Still, multimedia is an idea whose time has come. It desperately needs creative direction, and in the optimistic words of guru Ted Nelson, "must be controlled by dictatorial artists with full say on the final cut." It will invariably be supported by, but one hopes not led by, the technology that serves us—technology that László Moholy-Nagy termed "the reality of our century" nearly fifty years ago. "To be a user of machines," he wrote, "is to be of the spirit of this century." And so, in the spirit of this century, designers might give serious consideration to the contribution they owe to this new world: to the richness of texture, to the density of solution, and to the evolution of an information landscape that will support us all well into the next millennium.

4

TELEVISION CREATED THE MYTH OF THE GLOBAL VILLAGE. In a CNN broadcast in the spring of 1994, the President addressed the prospect of military intervention to restore democracy to Haiti. The network, which ascended to prominence when it televised the War in the Gulf some years back, proudly announced its "global" coverage of the President. Ironically, CNN is seen only in about 50,000 homes in Haiti—about one-tenth of its total population.

As a microcosm of the much touted (and increasingly maligned) "global village," this is a perfect example of the fallacy of digital communication: to date, personal access to information technologies remains largely a function of economics and privilege. Contrary to what many of us would like to believe, not everyone has a computer, or an internet address or, for that matter, a television. Such imperatives would seem to suggest great impediments ahead on the road to the information highway, and indeed there are: rather than forging new pathways between nations, modern telecommunications often take the form of preaching to the converted.

Still, in its most positive incarnation, the computer affords a kind of exchange virtually unprecedented in the history of communication. And nowhere is this more alarmingly present than in schools across the country, where technology-supported educational systems—particularly those that engage a student's participation in crafting his or her own curricula—activate an awareness of design issues at the earliest possible levels. The "classroom experience" has grown to include computer capabilities that, in turn, are revolutionizing the practices of teaching and learning. In an environment in which students collect information in multiple formats, they must organize, strategize, synthesize, and indeed—visualize. "Design" has become an integral function of everything they do and see and make.

Are we inadvertently breeding a new crop of "information architects"? Can a revolution in design education be far behind?

Today, a new kind of cross-disciplinary learning is made possible by interactive technologies: it is a process that invites the student's active participation in the identification, acquisition and synthesis of varied content. And with the advent of "multi" media comes a new kind of interpretive thinking. Such educational practices have virtually reversed the rhetorical paradigm of the Nineteenth Century classroom: in their place, a new educational initiative has emerged, one that focuses on authorship, scholarship and in the spirit of participatory media, reciprocity.

Efforts to better negotiate the equity gap between public and private schools remain the focus of certain concerned politicians—not the least of whom is former California governor Jerry Brown, who, as early as a decade ago, called for a "demonstration" school in each state that would devote itself to fully computerized instruction. Indeed, in the late 1980s, the California legislature called for a 30 million-dollar appropriation to insure that each student in the state—rich or poor—spent one hour per week in front of a video display terminal.

But California isn't the only state seeking progressive educational initiatives through technology. In Florida, the State Legislature and Department of Education have teamed up with Florida State University and Encyclopedia Brittanica to create *School Year 2000*, a cross-platform file server and software application that will provide students, faculty, administrators and parents with access to a wide array of information and data. In Rhode Island, Brown University president Vartan Gregorian is the key advisor on how philanthropist Walter H. Annenberg's $500 million gift aimed at improving public education will be spent: the nationwide challenge grants will go to support networks in and between schools, as well as to develop an electronic reference library that will eventually be available to every high school in America.

And from Nebraska, Senator Bob Kerrey presides over the executive board of the *New Media Centers* program, an international consortium of several hundred colleges and universities that team industry with academia to explore new, cross-disciplinary opportunities for using interactive media in higher education. Among the schools participating in this program are Stanford, where students are creating multimedia databases to study such topics as the history of Silicon Valley and Elizabethan theater; Princeton, where students are compiling 3-dimensional representations of seismic data for studying earthquakes and volcanoes; and Ohio State, where projects include archiving the world's largest collection of Asian and Buddhist art, as well as the development of a video archive documenting the choreographic accomplishments of Twyla Tharp.

So where, one might ask, are the design schools? And how are they revising their teaching methodologies—as these other schools are beginning to do—to respond to new media and to new thinking?

Many of the participating schools in the *New Media Centers* program are allocating funds and resources to investigate the uses of multimedia in community outreach programs. Students at Virginia Polytechnic Institute are focusing on the design of an internet site on the World Wide Web: their principal goal is to link the citizens of Blacksburg, Virginia with national and international information systems. At Eugenio Mariá de Hostos Community College in the South Bronx, the goal is to broaden learning opportunities through new media. Here, students focus on working with populations who historically have encountered significant barriers to higher education.

So, while the Jeffersonian model of equal access to all may remain a distant goal, these schools are proving that with the creative implementation of interactive technologies we can begin to address educational—if not social—change.

The Edison Project, Chris Whittle and Benno Schmidt's national public school initiative, is based upon a similar objective: the goal here is to build schools where "creativity, technological sophistication, motivation, responsiveness and accountability are the norm." Edison promises not only access to computers in the schools, but a computer in every student's home as well—an ambitious, though not impossible, undertaking. In the spirit of Schmidt's vision of marrying "creativity" with "technological sophistication," computer-aided classrooms all across the country are proving that such invention is indeed possible.

In New York, students at the Dalton School are designing HyperCard study kits about everything from the rain forest to astronomy to New York in the Civil War. Dalton's *New Lab for Teaching and Learning* supports technology at what are considered age-appropriate levels: here, multimedia is used to encourage multidisciplinary thinking. In a public high school in Columbus, Ohio, students also study in a technology-supported classroom environment that encourages investigation and creative growth. As one of a select number of designated schools in the *Apple Classrooms of Tomorrow* program (ACOT), these students not only participate intellectually in building their own curricula, but engage actively in their community as a result.

Both ACOT and Dalton are focusing on such collaborative, team-based projects. "In one such effort," recalls David Dwyer, ACOT's director and a distinguished scientist at Apple, "students created a scale model of the renovated business district in Columbus. They spent a month researching buildings, interviewing occupants and architects, and measuring and scaling skyscrapers to size. As a final product, they created a 20-by-20-foot scale model, including robotic elements they had built and programmed, controlled by a dozen computers. To share their effort with the city of Columbus, the students produced a videodisc, designed and built a HyperCard interface, and proudly displayed the model in the lobby of the city's museum of science and industry." These students are 12 years old.

In higher education, the initiatives are no less interesting. Graduate students at Cornell are designing hypermedia databases on cultural entomology: *Bughouse* is a field guide to insects and culture, incorporating video and animation, segments of old television commercials and movie clips, interviews and scientific data. Hypermedia fiction classes at Cornell and Brown focus on alternative storytelling techniques that involve visualizing new narrative structures. First-year law students at Harvard are creating research databases culled from findings on the internet, to study everything from torts to trial law (the latter being the basis for a seminar examining the O.J. Simpson defense).

The degree to which such study is made possible depends to a large degree on computer availability. According to *The Journal of Educational Computing Research*, the number of computers in schools has risen dramatically within the last decade, from an estimated 50,000 in 1980 to 2,400,000 by the early nineties. The University of Texas alone owns 18,500 computers, more than any other non-government-owned institution in the world. And it bears mention here that the academic community in general has been internet-aware since before many of us knew how to click a mouse. So is it any surprise that educators take a progressive view of technology-supported teaching and learning?

The race to technologize, however, has its detractors. In his book *The Cult of Information*, author Theodore Roszak argues that the discussion of education in the so-called "information age" has become distorted and biased. In his view, the emphasis on computers in schools is an abdication of true intellectual participation in a student's academic growth. Brenda Laurel concurs: though an avowed advocate of computers in education, she warns against the evangelical appropriation of technology in the classroom. "We must resist the temptation to see computer networks for kids as simply an alternative distribution channel for highly produced computer-game products," she wrote not long ago in an issue of *Edutopia*, the newsletter of the George Lucas Educational Foundation, "products that bring their own constraints, cultures, and implicit worldviews with them." In an ironic reversal of technology's claim to bridge socio-economic barriers through networked infrastructures, Laurel points out its equally dangerous potential for increased rarification, segregation and closure.

While students at Yale and CalArts and RISD gravitate to new media as an extension of their existing study, the advanced integration of cross-disciplinary learning remains the stronghold of universities who can support true scholastic diversity. What design programs offer, perhaps, is a more sophisticated understanding of design issues that help identify and shape the way we send and receive messages.

For graduate students in the Computer-Related Design course at the Royal College of Art in London, design itself is neither hardware nor software specific: the goal is simply to identify and solve a problem. Recent thesis projects included an interactive dream database, in which the designer focused on developing more flexible and intuitive ways of interacting with databases; a digital cooking assistant, which combined the "how-to" technique of the cookbook with speech recognition technology; "wearware," a technology-as-fashion experiment which included researching textile technologies to fabricate an interactive, dot-matrix fabric; and prototyping toolkits, including a wireless controller designed to facilitate product flexibility and user feedback. In an effort to lend their thinking to problems in a new environment, students questioned existing paradigms and the kinds of verbal, visual and ergonomic exchange they implicitly suggest.

43

What remains problematic is the degree to which design education addresses the fundamental changes brought about by new information technologies. With the emergence of the internet, individual voices struggle to be heard in a landscape ripe with convergence and collaboration. This is the "environment" in which design decisions, if they are to exist—and indeed, to succeed—must communicate. It is truly a culture of interruption, of perpetual change, and most of all, of reciprocity. As we have seen, educational initiatives in non-design related programs across the country encourage students to explore and help define this new language: are design educators rethinking how to better reconcile their curricula to correspond to—and prepare their students for—this thinking, and this culture?

A generation ago, social theorist Marshall McLuhan coined the phrase "global village," a borderless world in which communications media would transcend geographical, if not political boundaries. A decade later, Alvin Toffler referred to the electronic "cottage" and wrote of the computer as a kind of machine-hearth, an emerging totem of technological worship. Today, advances in telecommunications suggest that predictions such as these may not be far from the truth. In an age in which we have been groomed to transmit and receive only the most abbreviated signals, technology—in its many forms—has come to play an increasingly vital role in the dissemination of news and information. In this view, the computer services the abridged vocabulary of a modern vernacular.

Its relationship to interpersonal communication, however, remains unresolved. As the laws of supply and demand suggest the emergence of an increasingly computer-literate society, one thing is certain: communication itself is being dramatically redefined, and only to a small degree, so far, by designers. The role that design and designers will play remains to be seen.

Still, the vision that designers have traditionally contributed will most likely be in great demand: "Every discovery," Le Corbusier observed in his 1954 preface to *Modulor*, "must at some time have made use of the head, the eye, the hand of a person." As information overload tips the scales, the demand for editorial and design direction will become more and more critical. As the proposed information infrastructure continues to grow, so, too, will the public's dynamic participation in all types of media continue to build.

Would that design educators, and their students, might participate as well in the emergence of this new and highly interactive global community.

5

WILL THE INTERNET JEOPARDIZE THE TRUE VALUE OF DESIGN? In his recent book, *Being Digital*, Nicholas Negroponte observes that "the internet is interesting not only as a massive and pervasive global network, but as an example of something that has evolved with no apparent designer in charge, keeping its shape very much like the formation of a flock of ducks."

The truth is, here, nobody is in charge.

The internet is a dialectic hybrid: a utopian archetype at once pragmatic and mythical, borderless and structured, it is a potentially infinite space with no geographical, political or otherwise material boundaries. An international network linking an estimated 30-50 million people in more than 60 countries, the internet is the dream of better, faster, sooner (and eventually, cheaper) raised to an exponent—playing on our love affair with speed, and luring us into the trap of the quick fix. With its electronic language of e-mail and emoticons, its emphasis on brevity and abbreviation, the internet is the large-scale fulfillment of the culture of interruption that began with grazing at dinner parties and found its aesthetic home in the rapid-cut, short attention-span editing style of MTV.

Only unlike MTV, here the opportunity for artistic expression is negligible, owing to technological limitations that are fundamental to its entire existence. It invites comparisons to the early days of pre-cable, black and white television, when to get a good picture you crafted adhoc sculptures made of aluminum foil to your set top antenna. Here the design challenges may have little to do with design as we know it, and more to do with a kind of creative thinking that is best served by inventing new models: because while the aesthetic parameters may be restricted in a physical sense, the conceptual opportunities are wide open.

If we consider the internet as a kind of galaxy, then the web is its first inhabitable planet. Life on the web is made up of "addresses," which are colloquially spoken of as "web sites" and formally expressed in the odd nomenclature of watered-down computer code referred to as "URLs" (Uniform Resource Locators). URLs take you to Home Pages, a kind of graphic welcome mat for a web address. Home Pages are currently being introduced at the rate of 1000 a day on the web, and why? For one thing, they're cheap real estate. From a corporate perspective, they are a sound investment indeed: unlike the high cost and long lead time of producing a CD-ROM, net postings can be revised, reformatted and added to daily, hyperlinked to additional information, which can include sound and graphics as well as related texts and external databases. This affords an unprecedented opportunity to refresh content at a rate that doesn't necessarily correspond to a weekly or monthly or even bimonthly publication schedule. For designers in particular, the relationship between what is variable and what is constant introduces new challenges in an environment characterized by such unrelenting change.

But the metaphors that drive the design and editorial development of most of these web sites are limited in scope, button-intensive navigation schemes ranging from simulated shopping malls to urban streetscapes, hackneyed metaphors intended to suggest a familiar social fabric with which multiple users can easily identify. Alternatively, they dutifully mimic the form and structure of a paper publication, which is its own restrictive model. In this new world, the social patterns and behavioral ramifications of how — and why — users access this material will demand that we conceptualize time and space with more ambitious thinking, more inventive models, and, undoubtedly, more inspired design than presently exist.

So how will the theoretical and practical functions of design reinvent — and sustain — themselves in this new idiom?

An anecdote.

I'm spending the day in an executive boardroom on the outskirts of Washington, DC, consulting with a client about the design of an internet web site. For six hours we brainstorm about models. What are the conceptual dimensions of this new space? I offer excerpts from my list-in-progress, made up of observations that suggest what I believe to be a more intriguing direction: among them, an advent calendar (the peek-a-boo dynamic of clicking on links just to see where they go); a stationery bicycle (the playful duality of travelling while standing still); a bathroom wall (the participatory quality of a graffiti free-for-all) to name a few.

I am faced with visualizing the concept of building this place, an aesthetic, and increasingly psychological, challenge. I imagine castles and caverns, great ziggurat-like towers of modular rooms fulfilling the mysterious and unimaginably diverse needs of a million fictional net-surfers.

49

But what sort of place is this that we are inventing? And what criteria can we adequately rely upon to do so?

And most of all, if we build it—will they come?

Conceptually, this is as much a problem of city planning as one of information design. We are faced with the task of initiating construction in an environment that has no prevailing vernacular. I have an image in my mind of an architecture that sits on a flat plain, barren and empty, summoned by the click of a mouse before springing miraculously to life—much the way Dorothy's hallucinatory spin takes her from black and white to technicolor in *The Wizard of Oz*. Except that here, there's no point of departure, no landscape to refer to, no neighboring buildings to respond to, nothing but the promise of extensively networked phone lines to support the anticipated emergence of this new utopian culture.

It's a mild, December evening as the taxi winds its way down Massachusetts Avenue en route to Union Station. We pass the American University, the Bolivian Embassy, the Ritz Carlton. Lights from second floor windows reveal wood-paneled libraries and cubicled offices, shutters and chandeliers. Why can't my web site look like this? I want draping flags and limousines, the drama of an illuminated doorway, asphalt and tumult, depth and dimension.

Yet unlike the world we inhabit, the web knows no drama or scale. Here, variety is reserved for rapidly changing content, while form is of necessity restricted by what is technologically permissible: the carrying capacity of data lines (more commonly referred to as bandwidth) has yet to meet the promise of internet hopefuls who boast full-frame, full-motion, full-tilt experience. For now, this means Quicktime video in microscopic scale; interlaced images (the ones that flow in as though filtered through venetian blinds); limited typeface selections (one is essentially restricted to system fonts) in questionable sizes (there is at least a 6-point discrepancy between Macintosh and PC display size); and an unfortunate convention for designating hyperlinks, in which the linked word or phrase is in color (the default is blue), and bold, and underlined.

This color/bold/underlined belt-and-suspenders approach to design is a standard feature on the web, thanks to the group of forward thinking, though typographically malnourished, scientists at the University of Illinois who invented Mosaic, the father of all graphical browsers. Unfortunately, these early design decisions quickly became standard conventions, difficult to challenge or alter, and virtually impossible to reject. Thus, the legacy of the thin blue line will endure beyond software upgrades and data acceleration. It will become as intractable a feature of the web as are icons on the desktop. And ultimately, such restrictions breed a sameness that is perhaps the greatest dilemma for design as it seeks to define itself in this new world.

In this view, corporate identity must struggle to perform, to individualize itself in an environment that might best be described as homogenized. And yet it presents a distinct marketing conundrum: how do you reach this, the most eclectic demographic profile in history? There is no target audience on the web, other than vague statistics that tell us more men cruise the net than women (though probably not for long), and that the average net-surfer is young: a recent editorial in *The New York Times* estimated the median age at 23 and dropping fast. Conversely, there is said to be some indication of growth among the over-65 crowd, who have discovered a new kind of meeting place on something called *SeniorNet*. Indeed, at its best, the web is a bias-free environment, blind and otherwise impervious to the discriminations of traditional community interaction: a social utopia, if nothing else.

Not surprisingly, perhaps, factions of all kinds have sprung up all over the web, with sophisticated search engines that permit content providers to track usage and evaluate pertinent data: soon it will become possible to track users' browsing patterns, for example, an attribute that could have enormous consequences for the editorial design and planning of hyperlinks.

In the meantime, at the very least, we can estimate with some certainty the number of "hits" in a given day or week, a feature that has publishers and other content providers understandably optimistic. "Never has there been a way to observe people and groups so accurately and unobtrusively," noted Robert Wright in *The New Republic*, calling the internet a "promised land for amateur anthropologists." In this view, the aforementioned demographic ambiguity may soon be replaced by accurate statistical findings that will ultimately help to shape more meaningful communication on the web.

While the web is by definition wide open, the creative opportunities—at least in a formal sense—are restrictive indeed. To begin with, we are restricted typographically: users access the net through a variety of browsers, and have the option of invoking font preferences of their own that virtually obfuscate any design intention on the creator's behalf. Typesetting, while primitive from a visual standpoint, demands some rudimentary knowledge of HTML (Hyper Text Markup Language), the screen description language that is to the web what postscript is to desktop publishing.

HTML is an offspring of SGML (Standard Generalized Markup Language), which was developed at IBM (for lawyers), adopted by the Pentagon (for archival purposes), and ultimately accepted by the academic community, who resisted the restrictive typographic commands that did little to accommodate the literary imperatives of stanzas and verses and footnotes, for example. Interestingly, it was a group of concerned scholars—*not* designers—who rallied together as something called the *Text Encoding Initiative* to fight for guidelines that would address the coding of texts to distinguish poetry from prose. It took them six years, but the guidelines—1,300 pages of them—were published in early 1994.

Second, we are restricted technologically: awaiting more efficient systems for information transmittal, graphic information is often compromised by its inability to be seen without inordinate compression schemes. Pictures flow in at a snail's pace; additional media require the assistance of "helper" applications to be downloaded. And while higher speed phone lines are more expensive but more efficient ways to access the web, elaborate design remains penalized by sluggish transmission time, leaving the modernist design skeptic to rightfully assume that in this environment, less is indeed a bore.

We are, for such practical reasons, left with a scarcity of options—limited palettes and clumsy geometries—and, perhaps most of all, no way to anticipate what it is we're designing since there is no parallel universe between what we transmit and what others will receive. There are at least a dozen graphical browsers on the market, each with its own idiosyncratic modulation that will unpredictably turn the most considered typography into a system font nightmare. Add to this the fact that most designers work on a Macintosh platform, while the majority of internet users access the web from a PC: the aspect ratio is completely different for each, as the Mac relies upon a square matrix of pixels, while on the PC pixels themselves are rectangular in shape. Monitor configurations differ dramatically too, virtually destroying any color balance one might have intended, and an aesthetic wasteland soon begins to surface.

Conversely, designing within such intractable limitations may breed its own unique sort of style, one that future historians of early web design may view with more charity than I am able to muster as of this writing. It is easy to imagine screen composition software, a year or so from now, that will enable designers to create in a virtually code-free environment, rendering today's design decisions primitive (if not pathetic) by comparison. But for now at least, the very technology that enables information to be transmitted electronically is the same technology that limits its capacity to evolve as a truly interpretive medium. Ironically, it is this— not a person or an institution, but the technology itself—that ultimately governs activity on the internet. Referring specifically to the pervasive influence that the internet has had in academic circles over the past twenty years, a recent editorial in *The Economist* suggested that interactive technologies free certain kinds of text from the stronghold of academia, "just as books before them were freed from the church and the wealthy by printing." In this view, the internet offers perhaps the next in a step of evolutionary processes that redefine communication by freeing words and pictures from the conventions of the two-dimensional world, introducing a new language of form and function in which design may one day play a critical role.

6

WHAT IS IT THAT MAKES A STORY TRULY MEMORABLE? Over dinner recently, my mother recounted a passage from *The Alexandria Quartet*. Although her most recent reading had been years ago, her face lit up as she cited certain key moments—the names of characters, descriptions of settings, meaningful fragments of her own reading of this text. Her detailed recollections were delivered with enthusiasm and delight, a testament to the evocative durability of Lawrence Durrell's epic tale.

It occurred to me that I had never heard anyone describe an experience with interactive media in quite the same way. This book had meant something to my mother: one might even say that her reading of it had been interactive. Even had Durrell not structured the four volumes of the *Quartet* to be read in any order—an early, and by contemporary standards, crude, experiment in interactivity—I suspect she would have derived the same pleasure from his novels. My mother's references were personal, idiosyncratic; her interpretations specific to her own life experience. By choosing to read the story again years later, she had further enriched her experience of its narrative, its characters and setting, its unusual dimensions.

55

One of the great gifts of fiction lies in its ability to do precisely this: to transport us to a different time and place, an alternative space in which we make silent observations, imperceptibly casting ourselves inside a story's domain. We often experience a trip to the movies in a similar way. Captive in a darkened room, the immense scale of the screen exorcises any dueling reality, leaving our focus streamlined and our attention riveted.

Does this kind of mesmerizing interaction demand total darkness to fully enlist our attention? Or can interactive technologies—and their designers—hope to achieve a similar goal?

"Interactivity" with the screen has been, up until very recently, primarily a consequence of seeing and responding internally—viscerally, even—to a moment observed. For over a century it has remained the role of the writer, the director and cinematographer (and on occasion, the designer) to render a moment in time through plot and character, sound, motion and emotion. Over time, as technology grew to support greater complexity in film "making," so, too, did the variety of our reactions to the screen: pain and laughter, fear, terror, anticipation and excitement. The public's continued love affair with the movies is a constant reminder of the enduring power of the screen as an engaging, seductive, even hypnotic medium.

As we struggle to reconcile our conflicting reactions to information overload, the dramatic—and dynamic—model of filmic storytelling offers a more compelling way to think about the power of visual narrative. From scene to sequence, montage to mise-en-scène, visual staging on the screen has a long and distinguished history. Why has this rich legacy been virtually ignored in the design and development of interactive screen-based media?

Over the last decade, the growth of the consumer electronics market has introduced opportunities for designers ranging from on-air graphics to video games to a host of information services, requiring a skill that has come to be commonly referred to as interface design. Led (and occasionally restricted) by the technology that serves us, its visual vocabulary has emerged as a reductive pictorial syntax, an ironic casualty of late Twentieth Century modernism taken to an info-graphic extreme. Efforts to make complex information accessible to all have resulted in a new global language of sterile, stilted iconography: miniature hieroglyphs featuring cartoon-like facsimiles of task-driven processes, file folders and trashcans and most recently (and lamentably), emoticons. In earlier essays I have discussed what critic Andrew Olds dubbed an "ideogrammatic mode of organization," expressing my own dissatisfaction with what I have come to refer to as the desktop legacy: the icon-driven graphical language that is, to date, the dubious aesthetic hallmark of the so-called computer age.

Today, these intransigent emblems of consumer technology offer little leeway for expressing the greater complexities introduced by dynamic, time-based media. Better to look at the narrative models suggested by screens other than the computer: most notably, the silver one.

For the better part of this century, the designer's contribution to film has resided largely in the creation of title sequences. Like the shaping of information on a package or book jacket, titles are critical to our immediate perception of the underlying content. They bespeak, in a sense, the film's corporate identity: uniting form and content, they are uniquely, critically connected to our immediate responses, responses that are reflected in box office receipts and Oscar nominations and ultimately, the economic livelihood of the movie industry as a whole.

Yet even given some of the more inspired examples often cited in the design press, film titles dwell at the physical peripheries of the movies themselves. Ultimately, their role lies somewhere between the promotional and the propagandistic. Their principal duty is to introduce functional information rooted in contractual imperatives: billing and credits are serious business, particularly if you're the star and your agreement stipulates that your name precede the title of the film itself. In this view, the design challenge becomes a strategic mediation between storytelling and story *selling*.

This is not to minimize the impact that titles can and should have on a film's identity and the introduction of its narrative. Like the rigors evident in any other design process, good film title design reflects a significant understanding of content, and a clear ability to visualize that content into a dynamic form at once suitable and surprising. There is a choreographic component to all of this that demands an attention to the relationship between visual and aural stimuli, matching representative sequences to cuts from the film's soundtrack, for instance.

Still, the design of titles remains a highly controlled process. Yet more and more, as we enter a world in which the dissemination of information is controlled by a new and increasingly eclectic generation of viewers, the kind of thinking that once drove such one-way design decisions must be remodeled. With interaction comes choice, followed invariably by chaos—unless "good design" intervenes in the form of navigational support.

Actually, that's not true.

Interaction design is not only information design: it demands, instead, more comprehensive thinking that involves cognitive, spatial and ergonomic considerations. As richer, more complex content finds its way into the electronic sphere, the design challenges for shaping that content demand more than mere attention to directional clarity. Like the filmic model cited earlier, successful visual communication will become critically dependent upon our understanding of narrative, of audience, and of drama.

The classic Aristotelian definition of narrative is a story that has a beginning, a middle and an end. The traditional structuralist definition suggests that this breaks down to a two-tiered model of "story" and "discourse." In a contemporary variant on this view that may be more relevant to interaction design, critic Hamett Nurosi posits "the presentation of an event or a sequence of events that are connected by subject matter and related by time and space." His own bifurcated analysis suggests a deconstruction of narrative that subdivides between "story" and "storyteller." The early Twentieth Century novelist D.H. Lawrence held a more skeptical view. "Trust the tale," he wrote, "not the teller."

What happens when the story, by virtue of its distribution in a digital environment, becomes infinitely changeable? In time-based media, we no longer have control over hierarchical relationships. Communication is no longer rhetorical. Stories don't necessarily have a beginning, middle and an end. How do we design for such perpetual, and unpredictable interruption? If each viewer becomes the de facto storyteller, how do we maintain the integrity of authorship, the focus of plot, the lyrical cadences of a storyteller's voice and vision and point of view? As interactive technologies grow more complex, we are witnessing the emergence of a kind of shared authorship in which the linear parameters of classic narrative structure may no longer apply.

If, as designers, we are asked to consider the permutations of a story, our role typically has involved articulating the formal ways in which the story is rendered visually manifest. We think in terms of point and counterpoint, word and image, pacing and sequencing, cropping and juxtaposing. In this medium, however, we must devise new methods for visualizing stories in multiple layers, for designing with multiple points of entry.

One of these layers, of course, is visual. Another is textural. Another is informational. Still another is dramatic. There is time and motion and sound to be considered, and finally, there is "hypertext"—the ability to link ideas and images—which redefines the message transmitted by virtue of its connection to the message received.

The interpretive flexibility inherent in such new media suggests that point of view is itself a powerful narrative tool. Consider Akiro Kurosawa's 1951 film, *Rashomon*. Here, the spine of the story bases itself on a single crime that has been committed. The story is then told through the "viewpoints" of various characters. At once a rich tapestry of multiple perceptions, our attention is equally riveted by the telling of each individual story: multiple points of entry with a singular plotline. Each character in the film is an eyewitness: so, too, are we.

The concept of the eyewitness is central to thinking about the new visual narrative. It places the emphasis on the viewer, the end-user, the beholder of that information. It values the power of individual observation over the one-sidedness of oration, and, in so doing, makes the experience of viewing that much more memorable. It challenges traditional expectations of form and content, of author and audience, perhaps even of beginnings and endings. The audience, central to this interaction, is the protagonist.

The challenge to the designer, then, is to mediate this interaction. Film director Sergei Eisenstein, who was trained as an engineer and an architect, described his role as a visual storyteller as a "contrapuntal method combining visual and aural images." His objective was to reduce complexity to a "common denominator" on behalf of what he considered to be a singular audience. Though perhaps no longer applicable in today's multimedia market, Eisenstein's goal of representing the intricacies of human experience through a carefully articulated armature of audiovisual phenomena remains a timeless model for study.

With today's interactive products comes a new definition of audience: no longer passive, theirs is a new kind of authority, offering enhanced choice as well as enhanced participation. This emphasis on participation may be the most compelling aspect of interactive technology, yet it jeopardizes our classic notions of the linear presentation of narrative form. Will such participation breed chaos, or even contempt?

Such random, wanton "choice" may not, in the end, be a necessary incentive to viewer interest. The screen is, and has always been, an immersive medium: in the movies our participation with it may be passive in a physical sense, but our attention—visually, psychologically—is riveted because of its evocative capacity to draw us in.

This remains one of the most enduring legacies of film, and one that today's interaction "screen" designers would be well advised to consider.

+ 1

IDENTITY TAKES MANY FORMS, AND NOT ALL OF THEM ARE REAL. We are often endeared by children who, in the absence of mature logic, make observations that are at once poignant and preposterous. My one-year old son, for example, lacks the social and spatial understanding of figure/ground relationships, so that when he visits his grandmother and sees her collection of Nineteenth Century oil portraits, he waves eagerly to them, fully expecting them to wave back.

If applying human behaviors to two-dimensional objects is a function of childlike innocence, then how are we to explain the growing popularity of two and three-dimensional chat rooms, in which simulated social exchange is rendered through a primitive graphic vocabulary of recycled clip art and goofy characters?

Enter the avatar: a customizable "agent" originally conceived to maximize time by automating tasks on our behalf. Today's avatars actually "do" very little, but symbolize a great deal: as visualizations of our on-line personas, they are a social order unto themselves. In cyber-parlance, they dwell in "habitats" (so-called by Randy Farmer, the first to invent them) or "GMUKs" (Graphical Multi-User Konversations,) online environments which have been created to visualize social exchange by linking words to pictures, phrases to gestures, the cadences of casual conversation made graphically explicit on the screen.

Your avatar is your signature, your trademark, the symbol of your physical presence in the virtual world. Most challenging here are the subtleties of social interaction: essentially this means additional software designed to help you "edit" your avatar, either visually (as in the case of Time Warner's *Palace*, where you can colorize, morph or amputate from a picture-editing tool palette that sits adjacent to your browser) or emotionally (as in Microsoft's *Comic Chat*, where a "gesture wheel" helps you inflect surprise, happiness, or despair.)

One of the indisputable consequences of computer literacy is a boost in visual awareness: though it by no means suggests an educated eye, the truth is that computer users spend a lot of time staring at their screens. They experiment with software. They experiment with fonts. Recently, it seems, they appear to be experimenting with their own identities. If the popularity of these habitats lies in the opportunity to express oneself visually, does this make everyone a designer?

Herewith, some thoughts on the avatar as subject, as object and as design ideal.

AVATAR AS DEITY

Like the equally misappropriated term "icon," the word "avatar" means God. Both words suggest a form of worship one would be hard put to associate with computers. While online communities posess an intangible quality one might liken to religion, they differ in the extreme by having little if any ethical foundation. In his excellent book, *War of the Worlds*, cultural critic Mark Slouka suggests that what sets the real world apart from cyberspace is its reliance upon context: without context, he argues, ethical behavior is impossible. One might argue that design—and here I am referring to *good* design—could address this need for context, introducing formal parameters that help define an identity or create a space. But to deify design does it, and us, a great disservice: rather, I am suggesting that the language of design—the rigors that define our training and thinking as designers—be invoked in an effort to add to the quality of life, such as it is, in virtual places.

AVATAR AS PERSONALITY

Are avatars meant to represent us or are they meant to reinvent us? In her book, *Identity in the Age of the Internet*, social psychologist Sherry Turkle notes the emphasis upon personality re-construction encouraged by electronically linked environments. Indeed, habitat users may have hundreds of avatars: some are idiosyncratic, some pictographic, some iconoclastic. Typically, some of the most enduring avatars have been those associated with recognizable symbols of popular culture: cans of Spam, Winnie the Pooh, or Tarzan, for instance. Like a flexible wardrobe, avatars are changed with some frequency—sometimes mid-conversation—to reflect the user's mood or opinion or reaction to something. Occasionally an avatar's personality may be illuminated through its position on the screen or vis-à-vis its physical relationship to another avatar. Such graphic choreography is meant to simulate behaviors such as hiding, flirting, sleeping, or eavesdropping. The abbreviated language of e-mail works as a kind of counterpoint to this little dance, with acronyms like "BRB" ("be right back") employed to represent one of "RL's" ("Real Life's") many interruptions: answering the door, the telephone, one's e-mail, and so on.

As the de facto voices of our avatars, we are still tied to system fonts (lots of Geneva spoken here), chat room speak (acronyms aplenty) and the unfortunate bubbles and rectangles that are built into the software to lift and separate voices from one another on the screen. Imagine the potential for design if dynamically generated exchanges in chat rooms were represented by more sophisticated typographic models. Here, the "gesture wheel" would give way to interpretive variants such as size, scale and weight, color, drop shadows, and bracketed serifs. It would be a sort of visual onomatopoeia, an online version of *Parole in Libertà,* with words having their own distinct personalities.

AVATAR AS SUBCULTURE

Like icons, avatars succeed when they are simple enough to rasterize quickly: this means the images themselves are mostly flat, pixillized and cartoon-like, offering little opportunity for nuance or elegance or realism. Selecting which avatar to "be" is a kind of game, not unlike choosing a game piece in Monopoly, only habitat users have an additional choice to make: you can choose to publish your "av," which means that if I post my Betty Boop, hundreds of people can log on and decide to be Betty Boop too. The net visual effect, and consequent experience, is of seeing an environment populated by hundreds of people who look identical to one another, suggesting perhaps that there is indeed safety in numbers. It's a new homogenized subculture of anonymous, cookie-cutter characters. It's the Levittown of new media.

In his book, *The Fifties*, historian David Halberstam offers a detailed analysis of the early days of television and of the culture of mass identification with which it is often remembered. Advertisements, primitive by today's standards, were typified by an earnest spokesperson who endorsed a product and, in turn, symbolized the strength of its sponsor. Betty Furness was chosen to be spokesperson for Westinghouse because she embodied enviable (and visually compelling) qualities: she was pretty without being glamorous, confident without being intimidating. That millions of consumers came to identify with her made her something of a heroine, and sales of Westinghouse products boomed.

As commerce on the internet becomes easier and more common, the role avatars will play in our daily transactions might not be so different. Is this where designers will add value, employed by corporations to design avatars that embrace strategic design principles and re-emerge as crudely anthropomorphized corporate identity symbols?

AVATAR AS SCHIZOPHRENIC

By all indications, the fictional self becomes even more so when visualized in an iterative medium like cyberspace. In habitat parlance, "props" (think prostheses) are additive features that modify an expression or accentuate a gesture. In researching this article, I came across a doctoral dissertation by a social scientist who offered a thoughtful analysis of his own collection, which included, among others, the image of Hercules, one of the planet earth, and for his more light-hearted moments, an image of Sigmund Freud wearing a propeller beanie. (The beanie is a prop.) When online environments include image editing software, this means you can change or "prop" your avatar, to suit your mood. But what it really suggests is the opportunity to reinvent yourself at will, what Turkle refers to as "cycling through multiple identities" or "negotiating multiple roles." And while the idea of improvisational identities may seem entertaining at first, the encouragement of such behavior has serious social and psychological ramifications. Indeed, research shows a high volume of users with evidence of multiple personality disorder and paranoid schizophrenia.

AVATAR AS ANALYST

Putting a positive spin on it, Microsoft believes its *Comic Chat* and *Virtual Chat* software offerings serve a therapeutic social function, providing forums where participants can communicate while they are investigating identity issues. Skeptics might well question Microsoft's dubious foray into psychoanalysis, as I have. But real criticism should be reserved for the design of the product: *Comic Chat* turns conversations into comic strips, making it nearly impossible to imagine users discussing anything serious—the ethnic partitioning of Bosnia, for instance. Here, the "mood" is permanently preset: but isn't this an example of design overwhelming content? As chatting becomes visual, such software products—though fleeting—become visual artifacts, digital snapshots of contemporary culture. Most frustrating here is the selection of a single comic style (Microsoft chose Seattle-based cartoonist Jim Woodring), a restrictive choice that virtually disavows the impressive social, visual and political history of the comics. Why not draw from this rich history instead? Why Woodring and not Winsor MacKay? Or Chic Young? Or Ed Sorel?

The search for efficient self-expression lies at the heart of twentieth century aesthetics. In a medium that so clearly favors the terse, designers of avatars would be well advised to consider this appeal to minimalism. Rather than recycling fragments of popular culture (as the majority of avatar enthusiasts seem to do) why not look at Kasimir Malevich or at Robert Ryman? In the spirit of uniting man and machine, why not consult Oskar Schlemmer's 1928 costume designs for the Triadic Ballet? We might do just as well to read Ezra Pound or Upton Sinclair, whose commitment to verbal economy underscores the same distillation of means to convey a message. The reduction of pure form—circle, square and triangle—that was as compelling to Albers as it was to Cézanne would be well placed here, in the rectangle of the screen.

As avatars grow more common and complex, and more ambitious in terms of their ability to actually do things—to simulate conversational exchange, to exhibit dynamically generated behaviors—we will rely more and more upon visualization skills to establish online identity. The design challenges here are considerable: strategic, visual, conceptual, choreographic. At the moment, they are also extremely personal, making one question the need for design intervention at all. But if we step beyond the limitations of the medium, and take a broader view of the communities within which such social activity is taking place, we might imagine that the real design challenge lies in a more comprehensive approach: in this view, the designer may act much like a city planner, visualizing a functional system that addresses multiple social needs, and within which avatars of all shapes and sizes can peacefully coexist. In other words, envisioning context.

+2

THE UTOPIAN DREAM OF A PUSH-BUTTON WORLD IS UPON US. Lewis Mumford once wrote that he believed the industrial age was merely a passing phase in which the quality of human life would be sacrificed to further the prowess of technology. Today, as we near a new millennium, technology's legacy—and Mumford's prophecy—do indeed suggest a society utterly transfixed by its passion for speed. And most ironically in our impatient electronic culture, the phrase "Real Time" has come to symbolize the instantaneous, the nanosecond, or, what distinguished media oracle Marshall McLuhan once referred to as "allatonceness." Today, as we struggle to reconcile the virtual against the tangible, what does it mean to be real at all?

As it is, there is nothing particularly real at all about Real Time, and certainly nothing human about it. In electronic media, where the transmittal of data depends upon the generally unreliable support of varying bandwidth, Real Time is immediate time, everything at once time, time without interruption or delay. Real Time implies no waiting—but in the Real World, don't we occasionally wait for things? We wait in supermarket lines, at the bank, in movie queues; we wait "on hold" on the telephone, or put the VCR on "pause" to answer the door. Information transmittal, whether on CD-ROM or via networked phone lines or in face-to-face conversation, takes time. Delays, whether momentary or extended, are the casualties of such unpredictable transmittals and mirror the very real delays we face in everyday life. "Historical time is intermittent and variable," notes George Kubler in *The Shape of Time*, suggesting quite reasonably that indeed, life happens in between those moments. For electronic experiences to resonate with equal meaning, it would seem imperative for such lapses to be duly recognized, if not celebrated altogether.

Time takes many forms, and not all of them are real. There is psychological time, perceptual time, imaginary time, spiritual time. Social psychologists have observed that reality is made up of an amalgam of all of these. Noted sociologist P. A. Sorokin once observed that each culture and discipline has its own perception of time and its meaning: his definition of *socio-cultural* time is a conceptual model that lacks the distinguishing characteristics of horological time, using instead points of reference that are determined by unique social conditions. The irregular ebb and flow of time as it parallels human experience is a rich pattern marked by speed as well as slowness. By definition, the multifaceted nature of this concept prevents us from adopting a singular model for understanding the shape of time.

But by equating "real" with "efficient" we mistakenly perpetuate the idea that acceleration is the principal goal not only of performance, but of life itself. In so doing, we minimize both the value of human interaction and the potential for design to mediate that interaction. Real Time, in this context, is a misnomer: a more worthy definition comes from cognitive psychologist Donald Norman, who rightly observes that "real time is what humans do."

Like the concentric rings that indicate the age of a tree, the course of time takes many forms. Typically, we have come to recognize and respond to the kinds of visual codes that depict the gradual passage of time. While it takes only a fraction of a second to take a photograph, for example, the reverse side of a print from a photo library is stamped each time it is requested for publication, revealing, over time, a rich texture that bespeaks its long, productive life. Imagine if it were possible to build texture such as this in e-mail, or over the internet, or as a consequence of one's participation in a chat room. Yet as long as *digital* is understood to be *ephemeral*, the genesis of an idea—and its very rich evolution over time—will be impossible to visualize in quite the same manner.

Fake Time—or time as it currently exists—implies slower time. The implication here is that it is sluggish, retarded, anathema to the very acceleration that characterizes technological achievement in the Twentieth Century. Why is this non-instantaneous time not perceived of as reflective time? Or thoughtful time? Or quality time? Writing half a century ago of their disenchantment with the high-velocity life, poets such as T.S. Eliot and William Carlos Williams lamented the lack of tranquility and leisure in the face of emerging industry. Today, leisure itself has become such a rare commodity that it is deemed an area worthy of serious sociological inquiry—an anachronistic relic of our lost culture.

The visualization of time itself has always challenged designers, perhaps because the very unpredictability of its character precludes its being pummeled into any finite shape. And yet, for centuries humans have been trying to rationalize time, to harnass it into a form at once controllable and clear. Since the Fourteenth Century, the civilized world has measured time by the 24-hour clock. Agricultural societies and less technologically sophisticated cultures have typically operated in a similar manner, relying instead on the natural but highly regulatory movements of the planets. The seven-day calendar takes its cues from the movements of these celestial bodies, as the seven principal planets—beginning with the Sun and ending with Saturn—still provide the English (and French) speaking world with the etymological basis for its naming conventions. Human time-keeping systems are equally cyclical, if less apparently so: sleep rhythms and metabolic balances are as predictable as seasonal changes. Like the cycles that characterize planetary phenomena, such conditions can neither be anticipated, nor precipitated, nor accelerated at will.

While our current systems for mapping time have their roots in the Egyptian solar calendar, the rationalization of time that has come to characterize the modern world has evolved over numerous centuries and across multiple cultures. As a tool for managing time, the calendar itself offers a tabular system of temporal subdivision, enabling the rational and lateral compartmentalization of time. Seeing our weeks laid out in front of us, the assumption is that we can better control our time. Ironically, the great failure of the calendar lies in the homogeneity of its basic form: Monday is the same shape as Saturday, and June looks just like December. As the physical embodiment of this rationalization, the Filofax celebrates this efficiency by chopping time up into more digestible subdivisions, thus allowing us to conceptualize our days in "at a glance" modules of mornings or meetings or "to do" lists. Add to this the hyper-efficiency of electronic calendars and time management software, and time looks like its careening by even faster than it was the last time you checked.

Conversely, in time-based media the serendipity we pretend to enjoy is buried in a calculated process where all the permutations have been anticipated in advance. It is time-based because it is dynamic, but can it ever mirror the magical unpredictability and believable rhythms of real life? The basic economics of making interactive products depend to a considerable degree upon the technological wizardry of compression: speedy downloads are looked upon more favorably because they save us time, but the hidden danger here lies in truncating an experience as a consequence of doing so. This urge to race through information may explain why so much of the metaphor and visualization in new media takes its cue from game culture. Woefully overlooked here are the strategic games—chess, for example—that historically have had much more to do with human interaction and the speed with which such interaction naturally takes place. A better model might lie in the parlor games of the Nineteenth Century, board games and puzzles that were played at a slower and indeed, a more social pace. To date, such games demand a kind of reflective time which, though very real for those engaging in such activities, remains virtually ignored in the race to achieve Real Time nirvana.

Overlooked, too, are previous examples that successfully merged technology and society, addressing issues of social harmony and community interaction. Radio broadcasts half a century ago engaged and united audiences around boxes with plugs connecting them to an outlet in the wall. All radios did was deliver information electronically: they were tools for social congregation, valuable for their ability to disseminate a signal across the globe. But listening even today to the voices of Roosevelt and Churchill reminds us that the signal drew its real meaning from the rich cadences and intonation of the politicians themselves. Time compression would not have helped in the least: yet today, as we channel-chase and net-surf across the digital landscape, we are under the mistaken notion that we are richer for the experience of doing so.

Time itself is unquestionably our richest and most imperiled resource, underscoring everything we do and see and feel. If McLuhan was correct in his assumption that technologies achieve purpose when they extend humanity throughout the world, then our relentless pursuit of speed seems an illogical method for doing so. It is perhaps his more pragmatic observation that instantaneous electronic communication results in noticeable social disturbances that demands our immediate consideration: for designers, this means taking the time to rethink ways of visualizing messages to engage new and increasingly complex audiences.

It bears mention, too, that in studies of visual perception, two-dimensional images projected onto the retina only achieve full dimensionality as a result of our perception: we *infer* the third dimension of depth. Sadly, though, as the urgency to expedite all communicative transactions usurps our customary patterns of exchange, perception is accelerated as well. There doesn't seem to be a great deal of time left over to *infer*—or interpret, or imagine—much of anything at all.

In the end, of course, there is nothing real about this at all, except for our propensity to let it happen.

COLOPHON

THESE ESSAYS FIRST APPEARED IN *PRINT* AND *EYE* MAGAZINES.
This expanded edition is their first publication together in book
form, and updates an earlier edition published in 1995. The text is
set in Meta, a typeface designed by Erik Spiekermann in 1989.
Designed by Jessica Helfand and William Drenttel, this book was
imaged from a Macintosh file and bound in wrappers by Integrated
Book Technology in Troy, New York.